MOLIÈRE
OR
THE CABAL OF HYPOCRITES

Mikhail Bulgakov
Translated by
Richard Nelson,
Richard Pevear,
and
Larissa Volokhonsky

BROADWAY PLAY PUBLISHING INC
New York
www.broadwayplaypublishing.com
info@broadwayplaypublishing.com

MOLIÈRE OR THE CABAL OF HYPOCRITES
© Copyright 2021 Richard Nelson, Richard Pevear, & Larissa Volokhonsky

All rights reserved. This work is fully protected under the copyright laws of the United States of America. No part of this publication may be photocopied, reproduced, stored in a retrieval system, or transmitted, in any form or by any means, electronic, mechanical, recording, or otherwise, without the prior permission of the publisher. Additional copies of this play are available from the publisher.

Written permission is required for live performance of any sort. This includes readings, cuttings, scenes, and excerpts. For amateur and stock performances, please contact Broadway Play Publishing Inc. For all other rights please contact Patrick Herold, I C M.

First edition: June 2021
I S B N: 978-0-88145-834-3

Book design: Marie Donovan
Page make-up: Adobe InDesign
Typeface: Palatino

MOLIÈRE OR THE CABAL OF HYPOCRITES
premiered at the Moscow Art Theatre on 16 February
1936.

CHARACTERS & SETTING

JEAN-BAPTISTE POQUELIN DE MOLIÈRE, *famous playwright and actor*
MADELEINE BÉJART, *actress*
ARMANDE BÉJART DE MOLIÈRE, *actress*
MARIETTE RIVALLE, *actress*
CHARLES VARLET DE LA GRANGE, *actor, nicknamed "Recordbook"*
ZACHARIE MOIRRON, *actor famous for playing romantic leads*
PHILIBERT DU CROISY, *actor*
JEAN-JACQUES BOUTON, *candle snuffer and* MOLIÈRE's *servant*
LOUIS LE GRAND (XIV), *king of France*
MARQUIS D'ORSIGNY, *a swordsman, nicknamed "One-eye" and "Lord-have-mercy"*
MARQUIS DE CHARRON, *archbishop of Paris*
MARQUIS DE LESSAC, *a gambler*
THE HONEST COBBLER, *the king's buffoon*
CHARLATAN *with a harpsichord*
AN UNKNOWN WOMAN *in a mask*
FATHER BARTHOLOMEW, *a wandering preacher*
BROTHER FORCE, BROTHER FIDELITY, *members of the Cabal of the Holy Writ*
RENÉE, MOLIÈRE's *decrepit nanny*
A NUN
THE PROMPTER
MEMBERS OF THE CABAL *of the Holy Writ, in masks and*

black cloaks
COURTIERS, MUSKETEERS, *etc*

The action takes place in Paris during the time of Louis XIV.

Rien ne manque à sa gloire,
Il manquait à la nôtre.*

His glory lacks for nothing,
Ours was lacking him.

**Inscription on the bust of Molière installed in the Académie Française in 1778, a century after the playwright's death.*

ACT ONE

(From behind the curtain comes the muffled laughter of a thousand people. The curtain opens. The set represents the theater of the Palais Royale. Heavy curtains. A green poster with a coat of arms and ornaments. On it in big letters: "Players of Monsieur..." and some smaller words. A mirror. An armchair. Costumes. By the curtain separating two dressing rooms a harpsichord of enormous proportions. In the second dressing room, a very large crucifix, before which an oil lamp is burning. In the first dressing room, a door to the left, and a great many tallow candles [they evidently did not stint on light]. On the table in the second dressing room, only a lantern with colored glass.)

(On decidedly everything, on objects, on people [except for LA GRANGE*], the stamp of an extraordinary event, of anxiety and agitation.)*

*(*LA GRANGE, *not involved in the production, sits in his dressing room, deep in thought. He is wearing a dark cloak. He is young, handsome, and solemn. The lamp throws a mysterious light on his face.)*

(In the first dressing room, BOUTON, *his back to us, is pressed to the parting in the curtain. And even by his back it can be seen that the performance arouses a feeling of avid curiosity in him.* CHARLATAN *sticks his mug through the door.* CHARLATAN *puts his hand to his ear—he listens. Laughter is heard, then a final burst of guffawing.* BOUTON *seizes some ropes, and the sounds die out. A moment later*

MOLIÈRE *appears through the parting in the curtain and runs down the steps into the dressing room.* CHARLATAN *discreetly disappears.)*

(MOLIÈRE *is wearing an exaggerated wig and a caricatured helmet. He is holding a broadsword. He is made up as Sganarelle—a purple nose with a wart. Funny-looking. He holds his left hand to his chest, like a man with a heart ailment. The greasepaint melts down his face.)*

MOLIÈRE: *(Throws down the helmet, catches his breath)* Water!

BOUTON: Here.

(BOUTON *gives* MOLIÈRE *a glass.)*

MOLIÈRE: Phew! *(Drinks, listens with frightened eyes)*

(The door bursts open, DU CROISY *runs in, made up as Punchinello, his eyes popping out.)*

DU CROISY: The king's applauding! *(Disappears)*

PROMPTER: *(At the parting of the curtain)* The king's applauding!

MOLIÈRE: *(To* BOUTON*)* My towel! *(Wipes his forehead, nervous)*

MADELEINE: *(Made up, appears in the parting of the curtain)* Quick! The king's applauding!

MOLIÈRE: *(Nervously)* Yes, yes, I hear. I'm coming. *(Crosses himself by the curtain.)* Most pure Virgin, most pure Virgin. *(To* BOUTON*)* Open up the whole stage!

(BOUTON *first draws the curtain that separates the stage from us, then the immense one that separates the stage from the house. And now we see the stage in profile. It is higher than the dressing rooms and empty. The tallow candles in the chandeliers shine brightly. The house is not seen; all that is seen is a gilded loge at the edge, but it is empty. We only sense the mysterious, watchful blueness of the slightly darkened house.* CHARLATAN'S *face appears momentarily in*

ACT ONE 3

the doorway. MOLIÈRE *goes up to the stage, so that we see him in profile. He walks with a catlike gait to the footlights, as if stealthily, his neck bent, the feathers of his hat sweeping the floor. At his appearance, one unseen man in the house begins to applaud, after which there is thunderous clapping. Then silence)*

MOLIÈRE: Your…Majesty… Your Majesty. Most Serene Sovereign… *(He speaks the first words with a slight stutter—in life he stutters a little—but then his speech smoothes out, and with the first words it becomes clear that he is a first-rate actor. The wealth of his intonations, grimaces, and movements is inexhaustible. His smile is infectious.)* On behalf of the actors of Monsieur's company, your most faithful and most obedient servants, I thank you for the unheard-of honor you have done us by coming to our theater. And you see, Sire…words fail me…

(Slight laughter flutters in the house and dies down.)

MOLIÈRE:
Muse, my muse, O playful Thalia!
Every evening, heedful of your call,
By candlelight in the Palais-Royal, I…ah…
Put on my head the wig of Sganarelle.
Bowing, as is fit to do, quite low—
After all, it's thirty sous for the parterre—
To amuse Paris, O Sire, I must go
Pouring out stuff and nonsense everywhere.

(Laughter runs through the house.)

MOLIÈRE:
But tonight, O muse of comedy, I pray,
Come to my aid, come quickly, for you see
It's no small task, no small task, in a play
To get the Sun of France to laugh at me.

(The house bursts into applause.)

BOUTON: Ah, what a head! He thought up the sun.

CHARLATAN: *(With envy)* When did he write it?

BOUTON: *(Haughtily)* Never. Impromptu.

CHARLATAN: Is it possible?

BOUTON: Not for you.

MOLIÈRE: *(Sharply changes tone)*
You bear the royal burden for us all.
I am a mere player—a trifling thing.
But I play in your time, and so stand tall,
 Louis!...
   The great!!... *(Raises his voice)*
     French!!... *(Shouts)*
       King!!

(Throws his hat into the air)

(Something unimaginable starts happening in the house:)

VOICES: *(A roar:)* Long live the king!

(The candle flames are blown flat. BOUTON and CHARLATAN wave their hats, shout, but their voices are not heard. The broken calls of the royal guards' horns cut through the roaring. LA GRANGE stands motionless by his light, having taken off his hat. The ovation ends, and silence ensues.)

LOUIS: *(Voice. Out of the blueness)* I thank you, Monsieur de Molière.

MOLIÈRE: Your most obedient servants invite you to watch one more amusing interlude, if we're not boring you.

LOUIS: *(Voice)* Oh, with pleasure, Monsieur de Molière.

MOLIÈRE: *(Shouts)* Curtain!

(The main curtain conceals the house, and music immediately begins behind it. BOUTON closes the curtain

ACT ONE 5

that separates the stage from us, and it disappears. CHARLATAN's *face vanishes.)*

MOLIÈRE: *(Appears in the dressing room, muttering)* The bastard! ...I'll kill him! I'll cut his throat!...

BOUTON: Who does he want to kill in the hour of triumph?

MOLIÈRE: *(Seizing* BOUTON *by the throat)* You!

BOUTON: *(Shouts)* I'm being strangled at the royal performance!

*(*LA GRANGE *stirs by his light, but freezes again. At the shout,* MADELEINE *and* RIVALLE *come running in—* RIVALLE *almost totally naked, she was changing. The two actresses grab* MOLIÈRE *by the breeches, pulling him away from* BOUTON, *while* MOLIÈRE *kicks his feet at them.* MOLIÈRE *is finally torn away with a piece of* BOUTON's *caftan. They manage to throw* MOLIÈRE *down in the armchair.)*

MADELEINE: You're out of your mind! The whole house can hear you!

MOLIÈRE: Let me go!

RIVALLE: Monsieur Molière! *(She covers* MOLIÈRE's *mouth.)*

(The shocked CHARLATAN *peeks through the door.)*

BOUTON: *(Looking in the mirror, feels his torn caftan)* Beautiful job...and quick, too. *(To* MOLIÈRE*)* What's this about?

MOLIÈRE: This scoundrel...I don't understand why I keep the tormentor around. We've played it forty times, everything was fine, then the king comes and a candle falls from the chandelier, wax drips on the floorboards...

BOUTON: Maître, you yourself got up to your funny antics and knocked the candle over with your sword.

MOLIÈRE: Lies, you do-nothing!

(LA GRANGE *buries his face in his hands and weeps softly.*)

RIVALLE: He's right. You swatted the candle with your sword.

MOLIÈRE: The audience laughs. The king's surprised...

BOUTON: The king's the most courteous man in France and didn't notice any candle.

MOLIÈRE: So I knocked it over? I did? Hm... In that case why did I yell at you?

BOUTON: It's very difficult for me to say, sir.

MOLIÈRE: It seems I tore your caftan?

(BOUTON *pretends to laugh.*)

RIVALLE: My God, look at me! (*Grabs a caftan and, covering herself with it, flies off.*)

DU CROISY: (*Appears in the parting of the curtain with a lantern*) Madame Béjart, you're on, you're on, you're on... (*Vanishes*)

MADELEINE: Coming! (*Rushes out*)

MOLIÈRE: (*To* BOUTON) Take this caftan.

BOUTON: Thank you. (*Takes off his caftan and breeches, quickly starts putting on a pair of* MOLIÈRE's *breeches with lace ruffles at the knees.*)

MOLIÈRE: Ehh... And why the breeches?

BOUTON: Maître, you must agree, it would be the height of bad taste to combine such a wonderful caftan with these vile breeches. Kindly look: these breeches are a disgrace! (*Puts on the caftan as well*) Maître, I've discovered two silver coins of insignificant value in the pocket. How do you wish me to deal with them?

MOLIÈRE: How, indeed. I suppose, you crook, it would be best to put them in a museum. (*Corrects his makeup*)

ACT ONE

BOUTON: I agree. I'll do that. *(Pockets the money)* Well, I'll go and trim the snuff. *(Arms himself with a candle snuffer)*

MOLIÈRE: I beg you not to gawk at the king from the stage.

BOUTON: To whom are you saying that, maître? I, too, am courteous, seeing I'm French by birth.

MOLIÈRE: You're French by birth and a blockhead by profession.

BOUTON: You are a great actor by profession, and a boor by character. *(Disappears)*

MOLIÈRE: I committed some sin, and the Lord sent him to me in Limoges.

CHARLATAN: Monsieur director. Monsieur director.

MOLIÈRE: Ah, yes, you're here, too. I tell you what, sir… It's… Forgive me my candor—it's a second-rate trick. But the parterre public will like it. I'll put you on in the intermission during the week. By the way, how do you do it?

CHARLATAN: It's a secret, monsieur director.

MOLIÈRE: Well, I'll find out. Play a few chords, only softly.

(CHARLATAN, *smiling mysteriously, walks toward the harpsichord, sits on a stool some distance from it, and makes movements in the air as if he were playing, and the keys of the harpsichord go down, producing a gentle music.*)

MOLIÈRE: Damn! *(He rushes to the harpsichord, tries to catch the invisible threads.)*

(CHARLATAN *smiles mysteriously.*)

MOLIÈRE: Well, all right. Here's an advance. There's a spring somewhere, right?

CHARLATAN: Will the harpsichord stay in the theater overnight?

MOLIÈRE: Of course. You're not going to lug it home with you.

(CHARLATAN *bows and exits.*)

DU CROISY: *(Peeks in with a lantern and a book)* Monsieur de Molière. *(Vanishes)*

MOLIÈRE: Yes. *(Vanishes, and immediately after he disappears a roar of laughter is heard.)*

(The door-curtain leading to the dressing room with the green lantern is drawn aside and ARMANDE *emerges. The features of her face are lovely and resemble* MADELEINE's. *She is about seventeen years old. She wants to slip past* LA GRANGE.)

LA GRANGE: Stop.

ARMANDE: Ah, it's you, dear Recordbook. Why are you hiding here like a mouse? I've been looking at the king. But I'm in a hurry.

LA GRANGE: You have time. He's on stage. Why do you call me "Recordbook"? Maybe I don't like the nickname.

ARMANDE: Dear Monsieur La Grange. The whole company respects you and your chronicle very much. But if you wish, I'll stop calling you that.

LA GRANGE: I've been waiting for you.

ARMANDE: Why?

LA GRANGE: Today is the seventeenth, and I've put a black cross here in the record book.

ARMANDE: Has something happened? Has somebody in the company died?

LA GRANGE: I've marked it as a bad, black evening. Give him up.

ACT ONE

ARMANDE: Monsieur de La Grange, who gave you the right to interfere in my affairs?

LA GRANGE: Spiteful words. I implore you, do not marry him.

ARMANDE: Ah, so you're in love with me?

(Muffled music is heard behind the curtain.)

LA GRANGE: No, I don't like you.

ARMANDE: Let me pass, sir.

LA GRANGE: No. You have no right to marry him. You're so young. I appeal to what's best in you.

ARMANDE: The whole company's taken leave of its senses, I swear to God. What business is it of yours?

LA GRANGE: I can't tell you, but it's a great sin.

ARMANDE: Ah, the gossip about my sister. I've heard. Nonsense. And even if there was a romance between them, what is it to me?

(ARMANDE tries to push LA GRANGE aside and pass by.)

LA GRANGE: Stop. Give him up! No? Well, then I'll kill you. *(Draws his sword)*

ARMANDE: You're a crazy murderer. I...

LA GRANGE: What drives you to disaster? You don't love him, you're a young girl, and he...

ARMANDE: No, I do love him...

LA GRANGE: Give him up.

ARMANDE: I can't, Recordbook. We're lovers, and... *(She whispers in LA GRANGE's ear.)*

LA GRANGE: *(Sheathing his sword)* Go, I won't keep you any longer.

ARMANDE: *(Passing by)* You're a violent man. You threatened me. I can't stand the sight of you anymore.

LA GRANGE: *(Agitated)* Forgive me, I wanted to save you. Forgive me. *(He wraps himself in his cloak and leaves, taking his lantern.)*

ARMANDE: *(In* MOLIÈRE'*s dressing room)* Monstrous, monstrous...

MOLIÈRE: *(Appears)* Ah!

ARMANDE: Maître, the whole world's up in arms against me!

(MOLIÈRE *embraces* ARMANDE, *and at that same moment* BOUTON *appears:)*

MOLIÈRE: Ah, damn it all! *(To* BOUTON*)* Tell you what: go and see to the candles in the parterre.

BOUTON: I've just come from there.

MOLIÈRE: Tell you what, then: go to the barmaid and bring me a carafe of wine.

BOUTON: I've already brought it. Here it is.

MOLIÈRE: *(Softly)* Tell you what, then: just get the hell out of here!

BOUTON: You should have said that in the first place. *(He sighs heavily, goes to the door.)* Maître, tell me please, how old are you?

MOLIÈRE: What's that supposed to mean?

BOUTON: Some musketeers were asking me.

MOLIÈRE: Get out.

(BOUTON *exits.)*

MOLIÈRE: *(Locking the door behind him)* Kiss me.

ARMANDE: *(Hangs on his neck)* What a nose that is! You can't get under it.

(MOLIÈRE *takes off the nose and wig, kisses* ARMANDE.*)*

ARMANDE: *(Whispering to him)* You know, I'm... *(Whispers something in his ear.)*

ACT ONE

MOLIÈRE: My dear girl… *(Reflects)* Now there's nothing to be afraid of. I've made up my mind.

(MOLIÈRE leads ARMANDE to the crucifix.)

MOLIÈRE: Swear that you love me.

ARMANDE: I love you, I love you, I love you…

MOLIÈRE: You won't deceive me? Look, I already have wrinkles, I'm beginning to turn gray. I'm surrounded by enemies, and the disgrace would kill me…

ARMANDE: No, no! How could I do that.

MOLIÈRE: I want to live another lifetime! With you! But don't worry, I'll pay for it, I'll pay! I'll create you! You'll be the leading actress, you'll become great. That's my dream, which means that's how it will be. But remember, if you don't keep your vow, you'll rob me of everything.

ARMANDE: I see no wrinkles on your face. You're so brave and so great, you can't have any wrinkles. You're—Jean…

MOLIÈRE: I'm—Baptiste…

ARMANDE: You're—Molière! *(She kisses him.)*

MOLIÈRE: *(Laughs, then speaks solemnly)* Tomorrow you and I will be married. True, I'll have to endure a lot because of that…

(A distant noise of clapping is heard. There is knocking on the door.)

MOLIÈRE: Ah, what a life!

(The knocking is repeated.)

MOLIÈRE: We won't be able to meet at home, at Madeleine's, tonight. So here's what we'll do: when the theater lights are all out, come to the side door, in the garden, and wait for me. I'll bring you here. There's no moon.

(The knocking turns into a pounding.)

BOUTON: *(Shouts through the door)* Maître... maître...

(MOLIÈRE opens. Enter BOUTON, LA GRANGE, and ONE-EYE in the uniform of the Company of Black Musketeers, with a black band over one eye.)

ONE-EYE: Monsieur de Molière?

MOLIÈRE: Your most humble servant.

ONE-EYE: The king has ordered me to present you with his payment for a seat in the theater—thirty sous.

(ONE-EYE holds out the coins on a pillow. MOLIÈRE kisses the coins.)

ONE-EYE: But seeing that you labored for the king over and above the program, he has ordered me to make you an additional payment for the verses you composed and recited to the king—here are five thousand livres.

(ONE-EYE hands MOLIÈRE the money in a sack.)

MOLIÈRE: Oh, king! *(To LA GRANGE)* Five hundred livres for me, the rest to be divided equally among the actors of the company and handed out to them.

LA GRANGE: I thank you on behalf of the actors. *(Takes the sack and exits.)*

(In the distance a triumphant guards' march soars up.)

MOLIÈRE: Excuse me, sir, the king is leaving. *(Exits running.)*

ONE-EYE: *(To ARMANDE)* Mademoiselle, I'm very happy that chance... *(Coughs)* ...has given me the occasion... Orsigny, captain of the Company of Black Musketeers.

ARMANDE: *(Curtseys)* Armande Béjart. Are you the famous swordsman who can run anybody through?

ONE-EYE: *(Coughs)* You, mademoiselle, are no doubt an actress in this company?

ACT ONE 13

BOUTON: Here we go. Oh, my foolish maître!

ONE-EYE: *(Looks in astonishment at the lace on* BOUTON's *breeches)* Did you say something to me, my esteemed fellow?

BOUTON: No, sir.

ONE-EYE: So you're in the habit of talking to yourself?

BOUTON: Precisely so, sir. You know, once upon a time I talked in my sleep.

ONE-EYE: You don't say.

BOUTON: Yes, by God. And—it's so curious, imagine...

ONE-EYE: What the hell is this! Lord-have-mercy... *(To* ARMANDE*)* Your face, mademoiselle...

BOUTON: *(Insinuating himself between them)* I shouted wildly in my sleep. Eight of the best doctors in Limoges treated me...

ONE-EYE: And helped you, I hope?

BOUTON: No, sir. They gave me eight bleedings in three days, after which I went to bed and lay unable to move, taking holy communion every other minute.

ONE-EYE: *(Exasperated)* You're an original, my fine fellow. Lord-have-mercy. *(To* ARMANDE*)* I flatter myself, mademoiselle... Who is this man?

ARMANDE: Sir, he's the candle-snuffer—Jean-Jacques Bouton.

ONE-EYE: *(With reproach)* My dear fellow, I'll be delighted to hear about your shouting in your sleep some other time.

(MOLIÈRE *enters.)*

ONE-EYE: I have the honor of taking my leave. I'll run and catch up with the king.

MOLIÈRE: All the best.

(ONE-EYE *exits.*)

ARMANDE: *(To* MOLIÈRE*)* Good-bye, maître.

(MOLIÈRE *seeing* ARMANDE *out:*)

MOLIÈRE: There's no moon. I'll be waiting. *(To* BOUTON*)* Ask Madame Madeleine Béjart to come to me. Put out the lights and go home.

(BOUTON *exits.* MOLIÈRE *changes his clothes.* MADELEINE, *without her makeup, enters.*)

MOLIÈRE: Madeleine, there's a very important matter.

(MADELEINE *puts her hand to her heart, sits down.*)

MOLIÈRE: I want to get married.

MADELEINE: *(In a dead voice)* To whom?

MOLIÈRE: To your sister.

MADELEINE: Tell me you're joking, I beg you.

MOLIÈRE: No, God forbid.

(The lights in the theater begin to go out.)

MADELEINE: And me?

MOLIÈRE: You know, Madeleine, we're joined by deep ties, we're true friends, but we haven't been lovers for a long time...

MADELEINE: Remember when you were in prison twenty years ago? Who brought you food?

MOLIÈRE: You.

MADELEINE: And who has looked after you for these twenty years?

MOLIÈRE: You, you.

MADELEINE: Nobody drives out the dog that's guarded the house all its life. But you, Molière, you can drive it out. You're a terrible man, Molière, I'm afraid of you.

MOLIÈRE: Don't torment me. I'm in the grip of passion.

ACT ONE

MADELEINE: *(Suddenly kneels down and crawls towards* MOLIÈRE*)* But? But still...change your mind, Molière. Let's pretend this conversation never happened. Hm? Let's go home. You'll light the candles, I'll come to you... You'll read me the third act of *Tartuffe*. Hm? *(Fawningly)* In my opinion, it's a work of genius... And if you're in need of advice, who will you go to, Molière? She's a little girl... You know, you've aged, Jean-Baptiste, your temples are gray... You like your hot-water bottle. I'll make it nice for you... Picture it, a candle burning... We'll light a fire, and everything will be so good. And if, if you can't—oh, I know you... There's Rivalle... Not bad, is she? What a body! ...Hm? I won't say a word...

MOLIÈRE: Think what you're saying. What role you're taking on. *(Wearily wipes his sweat)*

MADELEINE: *(Getting up from her knees, beside herself)* Anyone you like, only not Armande! Curse the day I brought her to Paris!

MOLIÈRE: Hush, Madeleine, hush, please. *(In a whisper)* I must marry her... It's too late... I'm obliged to. Understand?

MADELEINE: Ah, so that's it! My God, my God! *(Pause)* I won't fight any more, I have no strength. I'll let you go. *(Pause)* I'm sorry for you, Molière.

MOLIÈRE: You won't deprive me of your friendship?

MADELEINE: Don't come near me, I beg you. *(Pause)* Well, so—I'll leave the company.

MOLIÈRE: Taking revenge?

MADELEINE: God knows I'm not. Today was my last performance. I'm tired... *(Smiles)* I'll start going to church...

MOLIÈRE: So you're adamant. The theater will give you a pension. You've earned it.

MADELEINE: Yes.

MOLIÈRE: When your distress subsides, I believe your feeling for me will return, and you'll want to see me again.

MADELEINE: No.

MOLIÈRE: You don't want to see Armande either?

MADELEINE: I will see Armande. Armande must know nothing. Understand? Nothing.

MOLIÈRE: Yes. *(The lights have all been put out. He lights a lantern.)* It's late, let's go, I'll take you home.

MADELEINE: No, thank you, there's no need. Let me sit here in your room for a few minutes...

MOLIÈRE: But you...

MADELEINE: I'll leave soon, don't worry. Go...

MOLIÈRE: *(Wraps himself in his cloak)* Good-bye. *(Exits)*

(MADELEINE *sits by the oil lamp, thinking, muttering. The light of a lantern is seen through the curtain.* LA GRANGE *enters.)*

LA GRANGE: *(In a solemn voice)* Who has stayed in the theater after the performance? Who's here? Is it you, Madame Béjart? So it happened, did it? I know.

MADELEINE: I'm thinking, Recordbook.

(Pause)

LA GRANGE: And you couldn't bring yourself to tell him?

MADELEINE: It's too late. She lives with him and she's pregnant. I can't tell him now. Let me be the only unhappy one, not the three of us. *(Pause)* You're a true knight, Varlet, you're the only one I've told the secret to.

ACT ONE

LA GRANGE: Madame Béjart, I'm proud of your trust in me. I tried to stop her, but I didn't succeed. No one will ever know. Come, I'll take you home.

MADELEINE: No, thank you, I want to be alone and think. *(Gets up)* Varlet, *(She smiles)* I've abandoned the stage today. Good-bye. *(She starts to leave.)*

LA GRANGE: Can't I still take you home?

MADELEINE: No. Go on with your rounds. *(Vanishes)*

LA GRANGE: *(Goes to the place where he was sitting at the beginning, sets down the lantern, which casts a green light on him, opens the book, talks and writes)* February 17th. The royal performance. In token of the honor, I draw a lily. After the performance, in the dark, I found Madame Madeleine Béjart in anguish. She is abandoning the stage… *(Sets down the pen)* The cause? A horrible event—Jean-Baptiste Poquelin de Molière, not knowing that Armande is not the sister but the daughter of Madame Madeleine Béjart, has married her, committing a mortal sin… That must not be written down, but as a token of the horror, I've drawn a black cross. And no one who comes after will ever suspect it. End of the 17th.

(LA GRANGE takes his lantern and exits like a dark knight. For a time there is darkness and silence, then in the cracks of the harpsichord light appears, there is a musical sound from the keys. The lid opens and MOIRRON *climbs out of the harpsichord, looking around thievishly. He is a boy of about fifteen with an extraordinarily handsome, depraved, and exhausted face. Ragged, dirty)*

MOIRRON: They're gone. Gone. To hell with all of you, devils, demons… *(Whimpers)* I'm a miserable boy, dirty…haven't slept for two days…I never sleep… *(Sobs, puts his lantern down, collapses, falls asleep.)*

(Pause. Then the light of a lantern floats up, and MOLIÈRE *stealthily leads* ARMANDE *in. She is wearing a dark cloak.* ARMANDE *shrieks.* MOIRRON *instantly wakes up, terror on his face, trembling.)*

MOLIÈRE: *(Threateningly)* Speak up, who are you?

MOIRRON: Monsieur director, don't kill me, I'm Zacharie, the miserable Zacharie Moirron...

MOLIÈRE: *(Bursting into laughter)* So that's it! Ah, that damned charlatan...

(Curtain)

END OF ACT ONE

ACT TWO

(The king's reception room. A multitude of lights everywhere. A white stairway leading no one knows where. At a card table the MARQUIS DE LESSAC *is playing cards with* LOUIS. *A crowd of courtiers, dressed with extraordinary magnificence, watches* LESSAC. *Before him lies a heap of gold; gold coins are scattered on the carpet. Sweat streams down* LESSAC's *face. Only* LOUIS *sits; the rest are standing. All are hatless.* LOUIS *wears the uniform of a white musketeer, a dashingly cocked hat with a feather, a military cross on his chest, golden spurs, a sword; behind his chair stands* ONE-EYE, *who directs the king's game. Beside them a musketeer with a musket stands motionless, never taking his eyes off* LOUIS.*)*

LESSAC: Three jacks, three kings.

LOUIS: You don't say.

ONE-EYE: *(Suddenly)* Excuse me, Sire. Marked cards, Lord-have-mercy!

(The courtiers freeze. Pause)

LOUIS: You came to play with me using marked cards?

LESSAC: Yes, Your Majesty. The impoverishment of my estate...

LOUIS: *(To* ONE-EYE*)* Tell me, Marquis, according to the rules of cards, how should I act in such a strange case?

ONE-EYE: Sire, you should smash him in the face with a candlestick. That's the first thing...

LOUIS: What a disagreeable rule. *(Takes hold of a candlestick)* This candlestick weighs about fifteen pounds. I suppose they should have set out lighter ones.

ONE-EYE: Allow me.

LOUIS: No, don't trouble yourself. And the second, you were saying...

COURTIERS: *(Bursting into a chorus)* Curse the dog!

LOUIS: Ah! Excellent! Be so kind as to send for him. Where is he?

(The COURTIERS rush in different directions.)

VOICES: The Cobbler! The king wants the Honest Cobbler!

LOUIS: *(To LESSAC)* Tell me, how is it done?

LESSAC: With the fingernail, Your Majesty. On the queen, for instance, I put little zeroes.

LOUIS: *(With curiosity)* And on the jacks?

LESSAC: X's, Sire.

LOUIS: Extremely interesting. And how does the law look upon these actions?

LESSAC: *(Upon reflection)* Negatively, Your Majesty.

LOUIS: *(Compassionately)* And what might be done to you for it?

LESSAC: *(Upon reflection)* I might be put in prison.

HONEST COBBLER: *(Enters noisily)* I'm coming, I'm running, I'm flying, I've arrived. Here I am. Greetings, Your Majesty. Great monarch, what has happened? Who do I have to curse?

LOUIS: Honest Cobbler, this marquis here was playing with me using marked cards.

ACT TWO

HONEST COBBLER: *(Crushed, to* LESSAC*)* You... So you... You...have you gone batty or something? Play like that in the marketplace and they'll push your face in. Did I give it to him good, Sire?

LOUIS: Thank you.

HONEST COBBLER: Can I have an apple?

LOUIS: Please help yourself. Marquis Lessac, gather up your winnings.

(LESSAC *stuffs his pockets with gold.*)

HONEST COBBLER: *(Upset)* Your Majesty, that's really... no, you're joking...

LOUIS: *(Into space)* Duke, if it's no touble for you, put the Marquis de Lessac in prison for a month. Give him a candle and a deck of cards—let him draw crosses and zeroes on them. Then send him—and his money—to his estate. *(To* LESSAC*)* Put the place order. And one more thing: don't play cards anymore; I have a feeling you won't be so lucky next time.

LESSAC: Oh, Sire...

VOICE: Guards!

(LESSAC *is taken away.*)

HONEST COBBLER: Out he goes!!

ONE-EYE: S-s-scoundrel!

(The VALETS *start bustling about and a table set for one appears before* LOUIS *as if from nowhere.*)

CHARRON: *(Emerging by the fireplace)* Your Majesty, allow me to introduce to you the wandering preacher, Father Bartholomew.

LOUIS: *(Starting to eat)* I love all my subjects, including the wandering ones. Introduce him to me, Archbishop.

(Strange singing is already heard outside the door. The door opens and FATHER BARTHOLOMEW *appears. First of all, he*

is barefoot; second, he is disheveled, belted with a rope, mad-eyed.)

BARTHOLOMEW: *(Dancing in, singing)* We are mad for Christ!

(Everyone is astonished except LOUIS. BROTHER FIDELITY—*sanctimonious physiognomy with a long nose, in a dark caftan—detaches himself from the crowd of courtiers and steals up to* CHARRON.*)*

ONE-EYE: *(Looking at* BARTHOLOMEW, *softly)* A spooky fellow, Lord-have-mercy!

BARTHOLOMEW: Most glorious king in the world. I've come to tell you that the Antichrist has appeared in your realm.

(Stupefaction on the COURTIERS' *faces)*

BARTHOLOMEW: The godless one, the poisonous worm gnawing at the foundation of your throne, bears the name of Jean-Baptiste Molière. Burn him on the public square, together with his godless work *Tartuffe*. All the faithful sons of the church demand it.

(At the word "demand" BROTHER FIDELITY *clutches his head.* CHARRON *changes expression.)*

LOUIS: Demand? Of whom do they demand it?

BARTHOLOMEW: Of you, Sire.

LOUIS: Of me? Archbishop, they demand something of me.

CHARRON: Forgive them, Sire. Today he obviously lost his mind. And I didn't know. It's my fault.

LOUIS: *(Into space)* Duke, if it's no trouble, put Father Bartholomew in prison for three months.

BARTHOLOMEW: *(Cries out)* Because of the Antichrist I suffer!

ACT TWO

(Movement—and BARTHOLOMEW *disappears as if he had never been there.* LOUIS *eats.)*

LOUIS: Archbishop, come here. I want to speak privately with you.

(The whole crowd of courtiers backs away to the stairs. The musketeer backs away, and LOUIS *remains alone with* CHARRON.*)*

LOUIS: Is he mad?

CHARRON: *(Firmly)* Yes, Sire, he's mad, but in his heart he's a true servant of God.

LOUIS: Archbishop, do you find this Molière dangerous?

CHARRON: *(Firmly)* Sire, he is Satan.

LOUIS: Hm. So you share Bartholomew's opinion?

CHARRON: Yes, Sire, I share it. Hear me out, Sire. Your cloudless and victorious reign has not been darkened by anything, and will not be darkened by anything as long as you love.

LOUIS: Love whom?

CHARRON: God.

LOUIS: *(Taking off his hat)* I do love Him.

CHARRON: *(Raising his hand)* He—is there, you—are on earth, and there is no one else.

LOUIS: Right.

CHARRON: Sire, there are no limits to your power and there never will be, as long as the light of religion rests upon your realm.

LOUIS: I love religion.

CHARRON: Then, Sire, I, and the blessed Bartholomew along with me, beg you—defend it.

LOUIS: You find that he has insulted religion?

CHARRON: He has, Sire.

LOUIS: The impudent actor is talented. Very well, Archbishop, I'll defend it... But... *(Lowering his voice)* I'll try to reform him, he may still serve the glory of our reign. But if he commits one more impudence, I will punish him. *(Pause)* This...blessed fool of yours...does he love the king?

CHARRON: Yes, Sire.

LOUIS: Archbishop, let the monk out after three days, but bring it home to him that when one speaks with the king of France, one must not utter the word "demand".

CHARRON: May God bless you, Sire, and may He bring your punishing hand down upon the godless man.

VOICE: Your Majesty's servant, Monsieur de Molière.

LOUIS: Let him come in.

MOLIÈRE: *(Enters, bows to* LOUIS *from a distance, walks past the greatly attentive courtiers. He has aged very much, his face is ill, gray.)* Sire!

LOUIS: Monsieur de Molière, I am dining, do you have any objections?

MOLIÈRE: Oh, Sire!

LOUIS: Will you join me? *(Into space)* Chair. Place setting.

MOLIÈRE: *(Turning pale)* Your Majesty, I cannot accept this honor. Spare me.

(A chair appears, and MOLIÈRE *sits on the edge of it.)*

LOUIS: What is your attitude towards chicken?

MOLIÈRE: My favorite dish, Sire. *(Pleadingly)* Allow me to stand.

LOUIS: Eat. How is my godson doing?

MOLIÈRE: To my great grief, Sire, the baby died.

ACT TWO

LOUIS: What, the second one, too?

MOLIÈRE: My children do not live, Sire.

LOUIS: You mustn't lose heart.

MOLIÈRE: Your Majesty, there has been no occasion in France when someone has dined with you. I am uneasy.

LOUIS: France, Monsieur de Molière, is here before you in this chair. She is eating chicken and is not uneasy.

MOLIÈRE: Oh, Sire, you alone in all the world can say that.

LOUIS: Tell me, what will your talented pen present to the king in the nearest future?

MOLIÈRE: Sire...whatever may...contribute to... *(He is nervous.)*

LOUIS: Your writing is witty. But you should know that there are subjects which must be touched upon with prudence. And in your *Tartuffe*, you'll agree, you have been imprudent. The clergy deserve respect. My writer could not be a godless man, I hope?

MOLIÈRE: *(Frightened)* Heavens no... Your Majesty...

LOUIS: Firmly believing that in the future your work will follow the right path, I authorize you to perform your play *Tartuffe* at the Palais-Royal.

MOLIÈRE: *(Gets into a strange state)* I love you, King! *(In agitation)* Where is Archbishop de Charron? Do you hear? Do you hear?

*(*LOUIS *stands up.)*

VOICE: The royal supper is over.

LOUIS: *(To* MOLIÈRE*)* Tonight you will make my bed.

*(*MOLIÈRE *snatches two candlesticks from the table and goes ahead. Behind him comes* LOUIS, *and it is as if a wind blows—everything gives way before him.)*

MOLIÈRE: *(Calls out in monotone)* Make way for the king, make way for the king! *(At the top of the stairs he calls into the void.)* You see, Archbishop, you can't lay a finger on me! Make way for the king!

(Trumpets sound loudly from above.)

MOLIÈRE: *Tartuffe* is authorized!

(MOLIÈRE *vanishes along with* LOUIS.)

(The COURTIERS *all vanish, only* CHARRON *and* BROTHER FIDELITY *are left on stage; both are black with rage.)*

CHARRON: *(By the stairs)* No. The king won't reform you. Almighty God, arm me and lead me after the godless one, so that I overtake him! *(Pause)* And he falls down these stairs! *(Pause)* Come here, Brother Fidelity.

(BROTHER FIDELITY *goes to* CHARRON.)

CHARRON: Brother Fidelity, what's the matter with you? Sending me a madman? You assured me he would impress the sovereign.

BROTHER FIDELITY: Who knew he would utter the word "demand"?

CHARRON: Demand!

BROTHER FIDELITY: Demand!

(Pause)

CHARRON: Have you found the woman?

BROTHER FIDELITY: Yes, Archbishop, everything's set. She sent a note, and she'll bring him.

CHARRON: Will he follow her?

BROTHER FIDELITY: The woman? Oh, you can be sure of it.

(ONE-EYE *appears at the top of the stairs.* CHARRON *and* BROTHER FIDELITY *disappear.)*

ACT TWO

ONE-EYE: *(Making merry by himself)* The preacher went fishing for the Antichrist and caught...three months in prison. True God, Lord-have...

HONEST COBBLER: *(Appears from under the stairs)* Is that you, Lord-have-mercy?

ONE-EYE: Well, let's say it is. You can simply call me the Marquis d'Orsigny. What do you want?

HONEST COBBLER: There's a note for you.

ONE-EYE: From whom?

HONEST COBBLER: Who knows? I met her in the park, and she was wearing a mask.

ONE-EYE: *(Reading the note)* Hm... What sort of woman was she?

HONEST COBBLER: *(Studying the note)* Of easy morals, I think.

ONE-EYE: Why?

HONEST COBBLER: Because she writes notes.

ONE-EYE: Fool!

HONEST COBBLER: What are you name-calling for?

ONE-EYE: Is she well built?

HONEST COBBLER: That you'll find out for yourself.

ONE-EYE: Right you are. *(Exits pensively.)*

(The lights begin to fade, and dark MUSKETEERS, *like phantoms, appear by the door.)*

VOICE: *(From the top of the stairs, drawls:)* The king is asleep.

SECOND VOICE: *(In the distance:)* The king is asleep!

THIRD VOICE: *(From underground, mysteriously:)* The king is asleep.

HONEST COBBLER: I'll sleep, too.

(HONEST COBBLER *lies down on the card table, wraps himself in a door curtain with coats of arms, so that only his monstrous boots stick out. The palace dissolves in darkness and disappears...*)

(*...and* MOLIÈRE's *apartment appears. Daytime. The harpsichord is open.* MOIRRON, *a very handsome, magnificently dressed young man of about twenty-two, plays tenderly.* ARMANDE *in an armchair listens, not taking her eyes off him.* MOIRRON *finishes the piece.*)

MOIRRON: What do you say about my playing, little mama?

ARMANDE: Monsieur Moirron, I've already asked you not to call me "little mama".

MOIRRON: First of all, Madame, I am not Moirron, I am Monsieur de Moirron. So there. Ha, ha. Ho, ho.

ARMANDE: Did you get your title for sitting in the harpsichord?

MOIRRON: Let's forget the harpsichord. It is covered over with the dust of oblivion. That was a long time ago. Now I'm a famous actor, all Paris applauds me. Ha, ha. Ho, ho.

ARMANDE: And I advise you not to forget that you owe it all to my husband. He pulled you out of the harpsichord by your dirty ear.

MOIRRON: Not by the ear, but by my no less dirty feet. Father's a decent man, no question, but he's jealous as the devil, and he has a terrible nature.

ARMANDE: I must congratulate my husband. He adopted an insolent twirp.

MOIRRON: I'm a bit insolent, it's true... That's my nature... But as an actor... No actor in Paris can match me. (*He is excessively cheerful, like a man who is asking for trouble.*)

ACT TWO

ARMANDE: Ah, how cocky! And Molière?

MOIRRON: Well...that goes without saying... There are three: the maître and me...

ARMANDE: And who is the third?

MOIRRON: You, mama. You, my famous actress. You're Psyche. *(Softly accompanies himself, declaims)* Through the spring forest... flies a god...

ARMANDE: *(Without expression)* Get away from me.

MOIRRON: *(Embraces* ARMANDE *with his left arm, with his right hand he accompanies himself)* How slim her waist... Amor the hero...

ARMANDE: His quiver brings... he aims an arrow... *(Anxiously)* Where's Bouton?

MOIRRON: Don't worry, the faithful servant went to the market.

ARMANDE: *(Declaims)* The goddess Venus love hath sent,/ Come, lover, ere its heat is spent.

(MOIRRON *lifts the hem of* ARMANDE's *dress, kisses her leg. She trembles, closes her eyes.)*

ARMANDE: Scoundrel! *(Anxiously)* Where's Renée?

MOIRRON: The old woman's in the kitchen. *(Kisses her other knee.)* Let's go to my room, mama.

ARMANDE: Not for anything, I swear by the most pure Virgin.

MOIRRON: Come with me.

ARMANDE: You're the most dangerous man in Paris. It was a bad hour, when we dug you out of the harpsichord.

MOIRRON: Come, little mama.

ARMANDE: No, I swear by the Virgin. *(Gets up)* I won't go.

(ARMANDE *goes, disappears through the door with* MOIRRON. MOIRRON *locks the door with a key.*)

ARMANDE: Why did you lock the door? (*Without expression*) You'll ruin me...

(*Pause*)

BOUTON: (*Enters with a basket of vegetables, carrot greens sticking out, sets the basket on the floor, listens*) Strange. (*Takes his boots off, sneaks up to the door, listens.*) Ah, the villain... But, ladies and gentlemen, I have nothing to do with it...I saw nothing, I heard nothing, I know nothing... Good Lord, he's coming! (*Vanishes, leaving the basket and his boots on the floor.*)

(MOLIÈRE *enters, sets down his stick and hat, looks perplexedly at the boots.*)

MOLIÈRE: Armande!

(*The key turns instantly in the lock.* MOLIÈRE *rushes through the door.* ARMANDE *cries out from behind the door, there is a scuffle, then* MOIRRON *comes running out, holding his wig in his hand.*)

MOIRRON: How dare you?!

MOLIÈRE: (*Running out after him*) You bastard! (*Gasping for breath*) I don't believe it, I don't believe my eyes... (*Sinks into the armchair*)

(*The key turns in the lock.*)

ARMANDE: (*Behind the door*) Jean-Baptiste, get a hold of yourself!

(BOUTON *peeks through the door, retreats.*)

MOLIÈRE: (*Shaking his fist at the door*) So you eat my bread and for that you dishonor me?

MOIRRON: How dare you strike me! Watch out! (*Grabs the hilt of his sword*)

MOLIÈRE: Let go of that sword, vermin!

ACT TWO 31

MOIRRON: I challenge you!

MOLIÈRE: Me? *(Pause)* Out of my house!

MOIRRON: You're crazy, father. A real Sganarelle.

MOLIÈRE: Disgraceful tramp. I warmed you in my heart, but I'll also fling you into the abyss. You'll act in fairground plays, Zacharie Moirron, from this hour on you're no part of the Palais-Royal company. Go!

MOIRRON: What? You're throwing me out of the company?

MOLIÈRE: Go away, my adopted thief.

ARMANDE: *(Behind the door, desperately)* Molière!

MOIRRON: *(At a loss)* Father, you imagined it, we were rehearsing *Psyche*…you don't know your own play… What are you ruining my life for?

MOLIÈRE: Go away, or I will stick this sword in you.

MOIRRON: So. *(Pause)* It would be extremely interesting to know who's going to play Don Juan? La Grange, maybe? Ho, ho. *(Pause)* But watch out, Monsieur de Molière, you may regret your madness. *(Pause)* I know your secret, Monsieur de Molière.

(MOLIÈRE *laughs.*)

MOIRRON: You've forgotten Madame Madeleine Béjart, have you? She's at death's door… She prays all the time… And meanwhile, Monsieur, France does have a king.

MOLIÈRE: Despicable, lying milksop, what are you driveling about?

MOIRRON: Driveling? I'll go straight from here to the archbishop.

MOLIÈRE: *(Laughs)* Well, thanks for the betrayal. I know you now. But know this, that if my heart might have

softened before those words, after them—never...
Clear out, you pathetic fool.

MOIRRON: *(From the doorway)* Damned Sganarelle!

(MOLIÈRE *grabs a pistol from the wall, and* MOIRRON *disappears.*)

MOLIÈRE: *(Shakes the door, then talks through the keyhole.)* Streetwalker.

(ARMANDE *sobs loudly behind the door.*)

MOLIÈRE: Bouton!

BOUTON: *(In his stocking feet)* Here I am, sir.

MOLIÈRE: Pimp!

BOUTON: Sir...

MOLIÈRE: Why are these boots here?!

BOUTON: Sir, it's...

MOLIÈRE: You're lying, I can see from your eyes that you're lying!

BOUTON: Sir, in order to lie one has to say something. And I have not yet uttered a word. I took my boots off, because... See these nails? They're hobnailed boots, damn them... So, you see, my feet clomped, and they were rehearsing, so they locked the door on me...

ARMANDE: *(Behind the door)* Right!

MOLIÈRE: Why the vegetables?

BOUTON: The vegetables play no part. None at all. I brought them from the market. *(Puts his boots on)*

MOLIÈRE: Armande! *(Silence. He talks through the keyhole.)* Do you want me to die, or what? I have a bad heart.

BOUTON: *(Through the keyhole)* Do you want him to die, or what? ...He has a bad heart...

MOLIÈRE: Get out! *(Kicks the basket)*

ACT TWO

(BOUTON *disappears.*)

MOLIÈRE: Armande!... (*Sits down on a low stool by the door.*) Bear with me a little while, I'll set you free soon. I don't want to die alone, Armande.

(ARMANDE *comes out with a tearstained face.*)

MOLIÈRE: Can you swear to it?

ARMANDE: I swear.

MOLIÈRE: Say something.

ARMANDE: (*Snuffling*) Such a playwright, but at home, at home...I don't see how they get along together. How? What have you done? It'll be all over Paris. Why did you throw Moirron out?

MOLIÈRE: Yes, true. A terrible scandal! But, you know, he's a scoundrel, a little viper...oh, a depraved boy, depraved, and I fear for him. Really, in despair he'll start dragging himself all over Paris. And I hit him... oh, how unpleasant...

ARMANDE: Bring Moirron back, bring him back.

MOLIÈRE: Let him wander around for a day, and then I'll bring him back.

(*Curtain*)

END OF ACT TWO

ACT THREE

(A stone basement lit by a three-candle chandelier. In a niche a communion chalice gleams. A table covered with red flannel, on it a Bible and some manuscripts. At the table sit MEMBERS OF THE CABAL *of the Holy Writ in masks. In an armchair, apart, without a mask, sits* CHARRON. *The door opens, and two sinister-looking men in black lead in* MOIRRON, *blindfolded, his hands bound. They release his hands and remove the blindfold.)*

MOIRRON: Where have you brought me?

CHARRON: That makes no difference, my son. Now, repeat your denunciation before this gathering of honest brethren.

*(*MOIRRON *is silent.)*

BROTHER FORCE: Are you dumb?

MOIRRON: *(Coughs)* I…holy archbishop…I didn't hear clearly then, and…maybe I'd better not say anything.

CHARRON: It seems, my son, that this morning you slandered Monsieur Molière to me.

*(*MOIRRON *is silent.)*

BROTHER FORCE: Answer the archbishop, you elegant trash.

(Silence)

CHARRON: It grieves me to see, my son, that you did slander him.

BROTHER FORCE: Lying's bad for you, my dear actor. You'll have to go to prison, pretty boy, where you'll spend a long time feeding bedbugs. And we'll proceed with the case anyway.

MOIRRON: *(Hoarsely)* I didn't slander him.

BROTHER FORCE: Don't prolong my agony: tell all.

(MOIRRON is silent.)

BROTHER FORCE: Ho there!

(Through the door come two MEN even more unpleasant-looking than those who brought MOIRRON.)

BROTHER FORCE: *(Looking at MOIRRON's shoes)* Pretty shoes you've got, but there are even prettier ones. *(To the torturers.)* Bring in the Spanish boot.

MOIRRON: No, don't. Several years ago, as a boy, I was sitting in the charlatan's harpsichord.

BROTHER FORCE: How did you wind up there?

MOIRRON: I played the keyboard from inside. It was a trick, as if the harpsichord was playing by itself.

BROTHER FORCE: And so.

MOIRRON: Inside the harpsichord... No, I can't, holy father...I was drunk this morning, I forget what I told you.

BROTHER FORCE: For the last time I ask you not to stop.

MOIRRON: And...at night I heard a voice say that Monsieur de Molière...had married...not the sister...of Madeleine Béjart, but her daughter...

BROTHER FORCE: In other words, my dear heart, you want to say that Molière married his own daughter?

MOIRRON: I'm not saying that, holy father.

ACT THREE

BROTHER FORCE: But I am. Don't you know that Molière lived for twenty years with Madame Madeleine Béjart? So whose voice was it?

MOIRRON: I guess I imagined it.

BROTHER FORCE: All right, whose voice did you imagine?

MOIRRON: The actor La Grange's.

CHARRON: That's enough, thank you, my friend. You have fulfilled your duty honorably. Don't torment yourself. Every faithful subject of the king and son of the Church should consider it an honor to denounce a crime that is known to him.

BROTHER FORCE: He's not so bad. I didn't like him at first, but now I see he's a good Catholic.

CHARRON: *(To* MOIRRON*)* You, my friend, will spend a day or two in a place where they will treat you well and feed you, and then you will go with me to the king.

*(*MOIRRON *is blindfolded, his hands are bound, and he is taken away.)*

BROTHER FIDELITY: So the king became godfather to a child of incest. Heh, heh.

CHARRON: Precisely, dear brothers. And we must not wish the man dead, for we are Christians, but we must try to reform the sinner by opening the king's eyes to him. A sinner sins for a long time and thinks that God has forgotten him. But the Lord remembers all. And society must be shown what Molière is, so that it turns away from him. For that, brothers, a stranger is about to appear, and I ask Brother Fidelity to speak with him, because the man knows my voice.

(A knocking at the door. CHARRON *pulls the hood over his face and disappears in semi-darkness.* BROTHER FIDELITY

goes to open the door. An UNKNOWN WOMAN *in a mask appears, leading* ONE-EYE *by the arm. He is blindfolded.)*

ONE-EYE: Enchantress, when will you finally allow me to take off the scarf? You might just trust in my word. Lord-have-mercy, your apartment smells damp.

UNKNOWN WOMAN: One more little step, Marquis... There... Take it off. *(She hides.)*

ONE-EYE: *(Takes off the scarf, looks around)* Ah! Lord-have-mercy! (*Instantly snatches out his sword with his right hand, and with his left a pistol, and stands with his back to the wall, displaying a great experience of life. Pause)* Some of you have sword points sticking out from under your cloaks. There may be enough of you to kill me, but I warn you that three of you will be taken out of this pit feet first. I'm Lord-have-mercy. Don't move. Where's the slut who lured me into this trap?

UNKNOWN WOMAN: *(From the darkness)* I'm here, Marquis, but I'm no slut.

BROTHER FORCE: No, Marquis, a lady...

BROTHER FIDELITY: We beg you to calm down, no one wants to attack you.

BROTHER FORCE: Put your pistol away, Marquis, it looks like a hollow eye, and spoils the conversation.

ONE-EYE: Where am I?

BROTHER FIDELITY: In the basement of a church.

ONE-EYE: I demand to be let out of here.

BROTHER FIDELITY: Any moment now the door will be opened.

ONE-EYE: In that case why have I been lured here, Lord-have-mercy? First of all—it's not a conspiracy against the king's life, is it?

ACT THREE

BROTHER FIDELITY: God forgive you, Marquis. Here we are all ardent admirers of the king. You are at a secret meeting of the League of the Holy Writ.

ONE-EYE: Bah! The Cabal! I didn't believe it existed. What does it need me for? *(Holsters the pistol)*

BROTHER FIDELITY: Sit down, Marquis, I beg you.

ONE-EYE: Thank you. *(Sits down.)*

BROTHER FIDELITY: We grieve over you, Marquis.

MEMBERS OF THE CABAL: *(In chorus)* We grieve.

ONE-EYE: I don't like it when people grieve. Get down to business.

BROTHER FIDELITY: We wanted to warn you, Marquis, that they laugh at you at court.

ONE-EYE: That's a mistake. I'm known as "Lord-have-mercy".

BROTHER FIDELITY: Who in France doesn't know of your incomparable skill? That's why they whisper behind your back.

ONE-EYE: *(Slapping the table with his sword)* Name names!

(The MEMBERS OF THE CABAL *cross themselves.)*

BROTHER FORCE: Why the noise, Marquis?

BROTHER FIDELITY: The whole court whispers.

ONE-EYE: Speak, or I'll lose my patience.

BROTHER FIDELITY: Tell me, do you know that most vile play by a certain Jean-Baptiste Molière called *Tartuffe*?

ONE-EYE: I don't frequent the Palais-Royal theater, but I've heard of it.

BROTHER FIDELITY: In that play the godless comedian has mocked religion and its servants.

ONE-EYE: Naughty boy!

BROTHER FIDELITY: But it is not only religion that Molière has insulted. Being a hater of the aristocracy, he has affronted it as well. Tell me, do you by any chance know the play *Don Juan*?

ONE-EYE: I've heard of that one, too. But what does Orsigny have to do with that carnival booth at the Palais-Royal?

BROTHER FIDELITY: We have absolutely precise information that the pen-pusher was portraying you, Marquis, as his hero Don Juan.

ONE-EYE: *(Sheathing his sword)* What is this Don Juan?

BROTHER FORCE: A godless man, a scoundrel, a murderer, and, forgive me, Marquis, a seducer of women.

ONE-EYE: *(With a changed expression)* So. Thank you.

BROTHER FIDELITY: *(Taking a manuscript from the table)* Maybe you'd like to acquaint yourself with the materials?

ONE-EYE: No, thank you, I'm not interested. Tell me, among those present might there be someone who thinks there were grounds for portraying Orsigny in this foul guise?

BROTHER FIDELITY: Is there anybody, brothers?

(Total denial among the MEMBERS OF THE CABAL)

BROTHER FIDELITY: There is no such person. So, kindly see what motives led us to invite you to our secret meeting in this strange way. Here, Marquis, there are people of your own circle, and you yourself understand how disagreeable it is for us...

ONE-EYE: Perfectly. I thank you.

BROTHER FIDELITY: Much-esteemed Marquis, we trust that what has been said today will remain between us, and no one will know that we have troubled you.

ACT THREE

ONE-EYE: Don't worry, sir. Where is the lady who brought me?

UNKNOWN WOMAN: *(Steps forward)* I'm here.

ONE-EYE: *(Grimly)* I offer you my apologies, madame.

UNKNOWN WOMAN: God will forgive you, Marquis, and I forgive you, too. Please come with me, and I'll take you back to where we met. Allow me to blindfold you again, because the esteemed society does not want anyone to see the way to their meeting place.

ONE-EYE: If it's really necessary.

(ONE-EYE's face is covered, and the UNKNOWN WOMAN leads him away. The door closes.)

CHARRON: *(Removing his hood and coming out of the darkness)* I declare the meeting of the League of the Holy Writ adjourned. Let us pray, brothers.

MEMBERS OF THE CABAL: *(Rise and softly sing)* Laudamus tibi, Domine, rex aeternae gloriae…

(An enormous cathedral filled with incense, mist, and darkness. Little lights wander about. The archbishop's small confessional with lighted candles in it. Two dark FIGURES walk by, a hoarse whisper is heard:)

FIGURE ONE: Have you seen *Tartuffe*?

FIGURE TWO: Have you seen *Tartuffe*?

(—And they are gone.)

(ARMANDE and LA GRANGE appear, leading MADELEINE under the arms. She is gray-haired, sick.)

MADELEINE: Thank you, Armande. Thank you, Varlet, my faithful friend.

(An organ begins to play on high.)

LA GRANGE: We'll wait for you here. That's the archbishop's confessional.

(MADELEINE *crosses herself and, having knocked softly, enters the confessional.* ARMANDE *and* LA GRANGE *wrap themselves in dark cloaks, sit on a bench, and are swallowed by darkness.*)

CHARRON: *(Emerges in the confessional)* Approach, my daughter. Are you Madeleine Béjart?

(The organ falls silent.)

CHARRON: I have learned that you are one of the most devout daughters of the cathedral. You are dear to my heart, and I myself chose to hear your confession.

MADELEINE: What an honor for me, a sinner.

(MADELEINE *kisses* CHARRON's *hands.*)

CHARRON: *(Giving her his blessing and covering her head with a cloth)* Are you ill, poor thing?

MADELEINE: I am, my archbishop.

CHARRON: *(Compassionately)* So you want to leave the world?

MADELEINE: I want to leave the world.

(The organ on high)

CHARRON: What is your illness?

MADELEINE: The doctors say my blood has gone bad. I see the devil and I'm afraid of him.

CHARRON: Poor woman. How do you save yourself from the devil?

MADELEINE: I pray.

(The organ falls silent again.)

CHARRON: For that the Lord will raise you up and love you.

MADELEINE: He won't forget me?

CHARRON: No. What are your sins, tell me?

ACT THREE

MADELEINE: I have been sinning all my life, father. I was a great harlot, I lied, for many years I was an actress and seduced everyone.

CHARRON: Do you remember committing some especially grave sin?

MADELEINE: No, I don't, archbishop.

CHARRON: *(Sorrowfully)* Foolish people! And so you come with a red-hot nail in your heart, and no one there will take it out. Never. Do you understand the meaning of the word "never"?

MADELEINE: *(Having pondered)* I understand. *(Frightened)* Oh, I'm afraid!

CHARRON: *(Turning into the devil)* You'll see fires, and amidst them...

MADELEINE: ...a sentry paces, paces...

CHARRON: ...and whispers...why didn't you leave your sin behind, why did you bring it with you?

MADELEINE: And I'll wring my hands, I'll cry out to God.

(The organ plays.)

CHARRON: And the Lord will no longer hear you. And you will slump down in your chains, and your feet will plunge into the fire... And it will be so forever. Do you understand the meaning of "forever"?

MADELEINE: I'm afraid to. If I did, I'd die at once. *(Cries out weakly)* I understand! And if I leave it here?

CHARRON: You will hear the eternal singing.

(On high a procession walks by with candles and children's voices sing. Then it all disappears.)

MADELEINE: *(Groping around with her hands, as if in darkness)* Where are you, holy father?

CHARRON: *(Toneless)* I'm here...here...here...

MADELEINE: I want to hear the eternal singing. *(Whispers passionately)* Long, long ago I lived with two men, with Molière and with another, and I conceived a daughter, Armande, and all my life I've been tormented, not knowing whose she was...

CHARRON: Ah, poor thing...

MADELEINE: I gave birth to her in the provinces, where I spent some time away from Molière. When she grew up, I brought her to Paris and passed her off as my sister. Then he, overcome with passion, became intimate with her, and I didn't tell him anything, so as not to make him miserable as well. On account of me, he committed a mortal sin. He may be living with his own daughter, and I've been thrown into hell. I want to fly up to the eternal singing.

CHARRON: And I, an archbishop, by the power vested in me, unbind you and set you free.

MADELEINE: *(Weeping with rapture)* Now I can fly?

(The organ sings out powerfully.)

CHARRON: *(Weeping happy tears)* Fly, fly!

(The organ falls silent.)

CHARRON: Is your daughter here? Call her in, I'll forgive her involuntary sin as well.

MADELEINE: *(Coming out of the confessional)* Armande, Armande, my sister, go in, the archbishop will give you his blessing. I'm happy...happy...

LA GRANGE: I'll help you into the carriage.

MADELEINE: And Armande?

LA GRANGE: I'll come back for her.

(LA GRANGE *leads* MADELEINE *into the darkness.*)

(ARMANDE *enters the confessional.* CHARRON *emerges, frightening in a horned mitre, and rapidly crosses*

ACT THREE

ARMANDE *several times with a reverse devil's cross. The organ drones powerfully.)*

CHARRON: Tell me, do you know who was with me just now?

ARMANDE: *(Horrified, suddenly understands everything)* No, no, she's my sister, my sister.

CHARRON: She's your mother. You're the daughter of Molière and Madeleine. I forgive you. But flee from him, flee from him today.

(With a weak cry, ARMANDE falls backwards and remains motionless on the threshold of the confessional. CHARRON disappears. The organ plays soothingly.)

LA GRANGE: *(Returns in semidarkness, like a dark knight)* Armande, are you sick?

(...Daytime. The king's reception room. LOUIS, in a dark caftan embroidered with gold, is at the table. Before him the dark and exhausted CHARRON. On the floor sits the HONEST COBBLER, mending a shoe.)

CHARRON: She confirmed it to me at confession before she died—and then I did not even deem it necessary, Your Majesty, to interrogate the actor La Grange, so as not to make too much of this vile business. And I stopped the investigation. Molière has stained himself with a crime. However, judge as it pleases Your Majesty.

LOUIS: I thank you, my archbishop. You have acted correctly. I think the case is now clear. *(Rings, speaks into space)* Summon Monsieur de Molière, the director of the Palais-Royal theater, at once. Dismiss the guards, I will speak with him in private. *(To CHARRON)* Archbishop, send me this Moirron.

CHARRON: At once, Sire. *(Exits)*

HONEST COBBLER: A kingdom can't exist without informers, eh, great monarch?

LOUIS: Hold your tongue, buffoon, and mend your shoe. So you don't like informers?

HONEST COBBLER: What's there to like? Such scum, Your Majesty.

(MOIRRON *enters. His eyes are harassed, he is frightened, and he looks as if he has slept without undressing. He is greatly impressed by* LOUIS, *whom he is obviously seeing close up for the first time.*)

LOUIS: *(Politely)* Zacharie Moirron?

MOIRRON: Yes, Your Majesty.

LOUIS: It was you who sat in the harpsichord?

MOIRRON: It was I, Sire.

LOUIS: Did Monsieur de Molière adopt you?

(MOIRRON *is silent.*)

LOUIS: I asked you a question.

MOIRRON: Yes.

LOUIS: He taught you the art of acting?

(MOIRRON *weeps.*)

LOUIS: I asked you a question.

MOIRRON: He did.

LOUIS: What motive guided you in writing a denunciation addressed to the king? It is written here: "wishing to serve justice".

MOIRRON: *(Mechanically)* Right, wishing...

LOUIS: Is it true that he struck you in the face?

MOIRRON: It's true.

LOUIS: What for?

MOIRRON: His wife was unfaithful to him with me.

ACT THREE

LOUIS: So. That need not be reported at an interrogation. You might have said: for personal reasons. How old are you?

MOIRRON: Twenty-three.

LOUIS: I announce to you some favorable news. The investigation has confirmed your denunciation. What reward would you like to receive from the king? Would you like money?

MOIRRON: (*Gives a start. Pause*) Your Majesty, allow me to join the king's players at the Hôtel de Bourgogne.

LOUIS: No. Our information says that you are a weak actor. Impossible.

MOIRRON: Me—weak?... (*Naïvely*) The Théâtre du Marais, then?

LOUIS: No again.

MOIRRON: Then what am I to do?...

LOUIS: What do you want with this dubious profession of actor? You're a man unstained. If you wish, you'll be taken into the king's service, in the investigative police. Submit an application in the king's name. It will be approved. You may go.

(MOIRRON *leaves.*)

HONEST COBBLER: A Judas, a Judas!...

LOUIS: Buffoon... (*Rings*) Monsieur de Molière.

(*As soon as* MOIRRON *vanishes through the door,* LA GRANGE *appears in another doorway, leads* MOLIÈRE *in, and at once vanishes.* MOLIÈRE *is a strange sight—collar askew, wig in disorder, sword hanging crooked, face leaden, hands shaking.*)

MOLIÈRE: Sire...

LOUIS: Why did you come with a companion, when you were asked to come alone?

MOLIÈRE: *(Smiling fearfully)* My faithful disciple, the actor La Grange...brought me. Please understand, I had pains in the heart, and I couldn't come alone... I hope I've done nothing to anger Your Majesty? *(Pause)* Please...a misfortune has befallen me...forgive me the disorder of my dress... Madeleine Béjart passed away yesterday, and my wife, Armande, fled from the house at the same time... Abandoned everything... Her dresses, imagine...a chest of drawers...rings...and left a crazy note... *(Takes a scrap of paper from his pocket, smiles ingratiatingly)*

LOUIS: The holy archbishop was right. You are not only a filthy blasphemer in your plays, you are also a criminal, you are—godless.

(MOLIÈRE *freezes.*)

LOUIS: I announce to you the decision in the case of your marriage: I forbid you to appear at court, I forbid you to perform *Tartuffe*. Only to keep your company from starving to death, I allow you to perform your funny comedies at the Palais-Royal, but nothing else... And from this day on, beware of reminding me of your existence! I withdraw the king's patronage.

MOLIÈRE: Your Majesty...this is a disaster...worse than the scaffold... *(Pause)* What for?!

LOUIS: For daring to ask me to stand as godfather to your child by your own daughter. For the shadow of a scandalous marriage cast upon my royal name.

MOLIÈRE: *(Sinking into an armchair)* Forgive me...I can't stand...

LOUIS: Leave. The audience is over. *(Exits)*

LA GRANGE: *(Peeking through the door)* Well?

MOLIÈRE: A carriage... Take me... Send for...

(LA GRANGE *vanishes.*)

ACT THREE

MOLIÈRE: Madeleine, advise me...but she's dead... What's happening?...

HONEST COBBLER: *(Sympathetically)* So, what is it you've done? You don't believe in God, right? ...Eh! you're really in a bad way... Have an apple.

MOLIÈRE: *(Mechanically takes the apple)* Thank you.

(CHARRON *enters and stops. Looks at* MOLIÈRE *for a long time. His eyes glitter with satisfaction. At the sight of* CHARRON, MOLIÈRE *begins to revive—before he was lying face down on the table. He rises, his eyes light up.)*

MOLIÈRE: Ah, holy father! Are you pleased? Is this for *Tartuffe*? I understand why you've rushed to the defense of religion. You caught on, my reverend sir. I don't dispute it. My friends once said to me: "One day you ought to portray some putrid monk". So I went and portrayed you. Because where could I find anyone more putrid than you!

CHARRON: I grieve for you, my son, because anyone who follows this path is sure to wind up on the gallows.

MOLIÈRE: Don't call me your son—I'm not the devil's son! *(Draws his sword.)*

HONEST COBBLER: Why the name-calling?

CHARRON: *(Eyes glittering)* But you won't even make it to the gallows.

(CHARRON *casts a sinister gaze around, and* ONE-EYE *comes from behind the door, holding a cane.)*

ONE-EYE: *(Silently approaches* MOLIÈRE, *steps on his foot)* Monsieur, you pushed me and did not apologize. You are a boor.

MOLIÈRE: *(Mechanically)* Forgi... *(Tensely)* You pushed me.

ONE-EYE: You're a liar.

MOLIÈRE: How dare you? What do you want from me?!

LA GRANGE: *(Enters just then, changes expression)* Maître, get out, get out this minute! *(Nervously)* Marquis, Monsieur de Molière is unwell.

ONE-EYE: I found him with a sword in his hand. He's well enough. *(To* MOLIÈRE*)* My name is Orsigny. You, my dear sir, are a scoundrel.

MOLIÈRE: I challenge you!

LA GRANGE: *(In horror)* Get out. This is "Lord-have-mercy".

CHARRON: Gentlemen, what are you doing... in the king's reception room... ah...

MOLIÈRE: I challenge you!

ONE-EYE: That's it. I won't insult you further. *(Sinisterly enjoying himself)* God be my judge, great king! Receive me, damp Bastille! *(To* LA GRANGE*)* You, sir, will be a witness. *(To* MOLIÈRE*)* Give him instructions about your property. *(Draws his sword, tests the tip)* No instructions? *(Cries in a low, drawn-out voice)* Lord-have-mercy! *(Makes a cross in the air with his sword)*

CHARRON: Gentlemen, come to your senses... gentlemen... *(Lightly flies up the stairs and watches the duel from there.)*

LA GRANGE: It's plain murder!

HONEST COBBLER: Cutting each other up in the king's reception room!

(ONE-EYE *grabs the* HONEST COBBLER *by the scruff of the neck, he stops talking.* ONE-EYE *falls upon* MOLIÈRE. MOLIÈRE, *warding him off, hides behind the table.* ONE-EYE *leaps on the table.)*

LA GRANGE: Throw down your sword, master!

(MOLIÈRE *throws down his sword, sinks to the floor.)*

ACT THREE

ONE-EYE: Pick up your sword.

LA GRANGE: *(To* ONE-EYE*)* You can't stab a man who has no sword in his hand!

ONE-EYE: And I won't. *(To* MOLIÈRE*)* Pick up your sword, you low-down coward.

MOLIÈRE: Don't insult me and don't fight with me. There's something I don't understand... You see, I have a bad heart...and my wife has left me... Diamond rings scattered on the floor...she didn't even take any linen... It's bad...

ONE-EYE: What is all this?!

MOLIÈRE: I can't understand why you fell upon me. I've seen you only twice in my life. You brought money? ...But that was long ago...I'm sick, please, don't touch me...

ONE-EYE: I'll kill you after your first performance. *(Sheathes his sword.)*

MOLIÈRE: All right...all right...it doesn't matter...

(The HONEST COBBLER *suddenly tears from his place and disappears.* LA GRANGE *picks* MOLIÈRE *up from the floor, grabs his sword, and leads him out.* ONE-EYE *gazes after them.)*

CHARRON: *(Comes down the stairs with burning eyes. Pause.)* Why didn't you kill him?

ONE-EYE: What business is it of yours? He dropped his sword, Lord-have-mercy!

CHARRON: Imbecile!

ONE-EYE: What!!! Filthy cleric!

CHARRON: *(Suddenly spits at* ONE-EYE*)* Tphoo!

*(*ONE-EYE *is so astounded that he spits back at* CHARRON. *The two go on spitting at each other. The door opens, the agitated* HONEST COBBLER *comes flying in, and after him*

comes LOUIS. *The two quarrelers are so carried away that they do not immediately stop spitting. The four stare at each other dumbly for a while.)*

LOUIS: Excuse me for interrupting. *(Vanishes, closing the door behind him)*

(Curtain)

END OF ACT THREE

ACT FOUR

(MOLIÈRE's *apartment. Evening. Candles in the candlesticks, mysterious shadows on the walls. Disorder, manuscripts scattered around.* MOLIÈRE, *in nightcap, underwear, and dressing gown, sits in an enormous armchair. In another sits* BOUTON. *On a table two swords and a pistol. On another, supper and wine, to which* BOUTON *puts his lips from time to time.)*

(LA GRANGE, *in a dark cloak, paces back and forth, half-humming half-murmuring something. He is followed by a dark knight's shadow on the wall.)*

LA GRANGE: That harpsichord...that harpsichord...

MOLIÈRE: Stop it, La Grange. You had nothing to do with it. Fate has come to my house and taken everything from me.

BOUTON: The veritable truth. I, too, have a tragic fate. For example, I used to sell little pies in Limoges... Nobody buys these little pies, of course. I wanted to become an actor, and I ended up with you...

MOLIÈRE: Shut up, Bouton.

BOUTON: I'll shut up.

(A bitter pause. Then a creaking of the staircase is heard, the door opens, and MOIRRON *enters. He is wearing not a caftan but some dirty jacket. Shabby, unshaven, and half drunk, with a lantern in his hand. Those sitting in the room shield their eyes with their hands. When they recognize* MOIRRON,

LA GRANGE *snatches a pistol from the table.* MOLIÈRE *hits* LA GRANGE'*s arm.* LA GRANGE *fires and hits the ceiling.* MOIRRON, *not surprised in the least, listlessly looks at where the bullet struck.* LA GRANGE *grabs objects at random, breaks a jug, falls upon* MOIRRON, *throws him to the ground, and begins to strangle him.)*

LA GRANGE: Hang me, King, hang me... *(Growls)* Judas...

MOLIÈRE: *(With suffering)* Bouton...Bouton...

(Together they drag LA GRANGE *off of* MOIRRON. *To* LA GRANGE:*)*

MOLIÈRE: You'll be the death of me, you...with your shooting and noise... What more do you want? To commit a murder in my apartment?

(Pause)

LA GRANGE: You creature, Zacharie Moirron, do you know me?

(MOIRRON *nods affirmatively.)*

LA GRANGE: Wherever you go this night, expect death. You won't see another dawn.

(LA GRANGE *wraps himself in his cloak and falls silent.* MOIRRON *nods affirmatively to him, kneels before* MOLIÈRE, *and bows to the ground.)*

MOLIÈRE: What have you come for now, my boy? My crime has been discovered, what else can you fish around for in my house? What more will you write to the king? Or do you suspect that I'm not only incestuous, but also maybe a counterfeiter? Go, search the cupboards and drawers. I give you permission.

(MOIRRON *bows down for the second time.)*

MOLIÈRE: Stop bowing and tell me what you want.

ACT FOUR

MOIRRON: My esteemed and most precious master, you think I've come to ask forgiveness? No. I've come to reassure you: by no later than midnight I will hang myself under your window, on account of the fact that my life cannot go on. Here's the rope. *(Takes a rope from his pocket)* And here's the note: "I am going to hell".

MOLIÈRE: *(Bitterly)* How reassuring!

BOUTON: *(Takes a sip wine)* Yes, a most difficult case. A certain philosopher said...

MOLIÈRE: Shut up, Bouton.

BOUTON: I'll shut up.

MOIRRON: I've come to be near you for a while. And if I did stay alive, I wouldn't give Madame Molière a single glance.

MOLIÈRE: You wouldn't be able to give her a glance, my son, because she's gone, and I'm forever alone. I have an impetuous character; I'll do something first, and only think about it afterwards. And so now, having thought and become the wiser after all that's happened, I forgive you and restore you to my house. Come in.

(MOIRRON *weeps.*)

LA GRANGE: *(Opening his cloak)* You're not a man, master, you're not a man! You're a rag to wipe the floor with!

MOLIÈRE: *(To* LA GRANGE*)* Insolent pup! Don't talk about what you don't understand! *(Pause. To* MOIRRON*)* Stand up, you'll wear holes in your trousers!

(Pause. MOIRRON *gets up. Pause)*

MOLIÈRE: Where's your caftan?

MOIRRON: I pawned it in a tavern.

MOLIÈRE: For how much?

(MOIRRON *waves his hand.*)

MOLIÈRE: *(Grumbles)* That's swinishness—leaving satin caftans in taverns. *(To* BOUTON*)* Buy back the caftan! *(To* MOIRRON*)* They say you went wandering around and even wandered into the king.

MOIRRON: *(Beating himself on the chest)* And the king said to me: spy, spy... You're a bad actor, he says...

MOLIÈRE: Ah, the human heart! Ah, my friend, my king! The king's mistaken: you're a first-rate actor, and you're no good as a spy, your heart's not in it. The only thing I regret is that I won't have very long to act with you. They've set a one-eyed dog of a musketeer on me, my son. The king has withdrawn his patronage, and they'll kill me. I've got to flee.

MOIRRON: Master, as long as I'm alive, he's not going to kill you, believe me. You know what a swordsman I am.

LA GRANGE: *(Sticks his ear out of his cloak)* You're an astonishing swordsman, true. But, you vile vermin, before you get near "Lord-have-mercy", buy yourself a funeral service in the cathedral.

MOIRRON: I'll stab him in the back.

LA GRANGE: That's just like you.

MOIRRON: *(To* MOLIÈRE*)* I'll never leave your side, at home, in the street, night and day. That's why I've come.

LA GRANGE: Like a spy.

MOLIÈRE: *(To* LA GRANGE*)* Stuff your mouth with lace.

MOIRRON: Dear Recordbook, don't insult me. Why insult a man who has no right to answer you back? You shouldn't touch me, there's a stain on me. And don't attack me tonight. You'll kill me, they'll hang you, and the Cabal will put the sword to our defenseless maître.

ACT FOUR

MOLIÈRE: You've grown considerably wiser since you disappeared from home.

MOIRRON: *(To* LA GRANGE*)* Bear in mind that the maître was declared godless for *Tartuffe*. I was there in the basement of the Cabal... He is outside the law, which means—expect anything.

MOLIÈRE: I know. *(Gives a start)* Did somebody knock?

MOIRRON: No. *(To* LA GRANGE*)* Take the pistol and a lantern, we'll go and keep watch.

*(*LA GRANGE *and* MOIRRON *take swords and a lantern and leave. Pause)*

MOLIÈRE: A tyrant, a tyrant...

BOUTON: Who are you talking about, maître?

MOLIÈRE: About the king of France...

BOUTON: Quiet!

MOLIÈRE: About Louis the Great! A tyrant!

BOUTON: That's it. We're both hanged.

MOLIÈRE: Oh, Bouton, today I nearly died of fright. A golden idol, and the eyes, would you believe it, were emeralds. My hands were covered in cold sweat. Everything started swimming askew, sideways, and I knew only one thing—that it was crushing me! The idol!

BOUTON: Both hanged, and I'm one of them. Side by side in the square. You're hanging here, and I'm kitty-corner. The guiltlessly perished Jean-Jacques Bouton. Where am I? In heaven. I don't recognize the surroundings.

MOLIÈRE: All my life I've been licking his spurs and thinking just one thing: don't crush me. And all the same—he crushed me! Tyrant!

BOUTON: And the drum beats in the square. Who stuck his tongue out at the wrong moment? It'll hang down to his waist.

MOLIÈRE: What for? You see, this morning I ask him, what for? I don't understand...I say to him: Your Majesty, I really hate such acts, I protest, I am insulted, Your Majesty, please explain... Please...maybe I didn't flatter you enough? Maybe I didn't grovel enough? ... Your Majesty, where will you find another kiss-ass like Molière? But what for, Bouton? For *Tartuffe*. For that I humiliated myself. I thought I'd find an ally. And that I did! Don't humiliate yourself, Bouton. I hate lawless tyranny!

BOUTON: They'll set up a monument to you, maître. A girl by a fountain and water spurting from her mouth. You're a distinguished man...just keep quiet... May his tongue wither... Why do you want to ruin me?

MOLIÈRE: What more must I do to show I'm a worm? But you see, Your Majesty, I'm a writer, I think... and I protest, she's not my daughter. *(To* BOUTON*)* Ask Madeleine Béjart to come here, I want her advice.

BOUTON: What are you saying, maître?!

MOLIÈRE: Ah...she died... Why, old girl, didn't you tell me the whole truth? ...Or, no, why, why didn't you shape me, why didn't you beat me... You see, she says, we'll light candles...I'll come to you. *(In anguish)* The candles are burning, but she's not here...I tore your caftan? ...Here's money for the caftan.

BOUTON: *(Tearfully)* I'll call somebody. That was ten years ago, what are you...

MOLIÈRE: Pack everything up. Tomorrow I'll play for the last time, and we'll flee to England. How stupid. It's windy on the sea, it's a foreign language, and generally it's not about England, it's about...

ACT FOUR 59

(The door opens and the head of old RENÉE *appears in it.)*

RENÉE: There's a nun come to see you.

MOLIÈRE: *(Frightened)* What's that? ...What nun?

RENÉE: You yourself wanted to give her the theater costumes to launder.

MOLIÈRE: Pah, you old fool, Renée, how you frightened me! Eh! Costumes! Tell her to come to the Palais-Royal tomorrow at the end of the performance. Fool!

RENÉE: Me? It was you who ordered it.

MOLIÈRE: I ordered nothing.

*(*RENÉE *vanishes. Pause)*

MOLIÈRE: So, any other business? Ah, yes, the caftan... Show me, where did I tear it?

BOUTON: Maître, go to bed, for God's sake. What caftan?

*(*MOLIÈRE *suddenly gets under the blanket and pulls it up over his head.)*

BOUTON: Almighty God, make it so that nobody heard what he said. Let's play a trick. *(In an unnaturally loud and false voice, as if continuing a conversation)* So what are you saying, my dear sir? That our king is the best, the most magnificent king in the whole world? You'll get no objections from me. I share your opinion.

MOLIÈRE: *(From under the blanket)* Giftless nonentity!

BOUTON: Quiet! *(In a false voice.)* Yes, I shouted before, I shout now, and I will always shout: Long live the king!

(A knock on the window. Alarmed, MOLIÈRE *sticks his head out from under the blanket.* BOUTON *cautiously opens the window, and the alarmed* MOIRRON *appears in it with a lantern.)*

MOIRRON: Who shouted? What's going on?

BOUTON: Nothing's going on. Why must something necessarily be going on? I was conversing with Monsieur de Molière and shouted: Long live the king! Doesn't Bouton have the right to shout something? So he shouted: Long live the king!

MOLIÈRE: God, what a giftless fool!

(...*The actors' dressing rooms in the Palais-Royal. The old green poster hangs in the same place as before, there is the same green lantern in* LA GRANGE's *room, and the oil lamp burns before the crucifix. But there is loud noise and whistling beyond the curtain.* MOLIÈRE *sits in an armchair in a dressing gown and nightcap, made up and with a caricature nose.* MOLIÈRE *is excited, in a strange state, as if drunk. Next to him, in black doctor's clothes, but without makeup, stand* LA GRANGE *and* DU CROISY. *Caricature doctor's masks are scattered about. The door opens and* BOUTON *rushes in. At the beginning of the scene,* MOIRRON *stands at a distance, immobile, in a black cloak.*)

MOLIÈRE: Well? Is he dead?

BOUTON: *(To* LA GRANGE*)* The sword went...

MOLIÈRE: I ask that you address the director of the Palais-Royal, not the actors. I am still in charge at the last performance!

BOUTON: *(To him)* Yes, he's dead. The sword went through his heart.

MOLIÈRE: God rest his soul. Well, there's nothing to be done.

PROMPTER: *(Peeking through the door)* What's going on?

LA GRANGE: *(Emphatically loud)* What's going on? Musketeers broke into the theater and killed the doorkeeper.

PROMPTER: Ohh... My God... *(Vanishes)*

ACT FOUR

LA GRANGE: I, the secretary of the theater, announce: the theater is full of musketeers and unknown persons without tickets. I am powerless to control them, and I forbid the continuation of the performance.

MOLIÈRE: But...but...but! ...He forbids! Don't forget who you are! You're a little boy compared to me. Look at my gray hair.

LA GRANGE: *(Whispers to* BOUTON*)* Has he been drinking?

BOUTON: Not a drop.

MOLIÈRE: What else did I want to say?

BOUTON: My golden Monsieur de Molière...

MOLIÈRE: Bouton!...

BOUTON: ..."get out!"...I know. I've been with you for twenty years, and all I've ever heard is that phrase, or "Shut up, Bouton" —and I'm used to it. You love me, maître, and in the name of that love I beg you on bended knee not to finish the performance, but to flee—the carriage is waiting.

MOLIÈRE: What makes you think I love you? You're a babbler. Nobody loves me. Everybody torments me and annoys me, they all pursue me. And the archbishop has issued an order not to bury me in the cemetery...so everybody will be within the pale, and I'll croak outside. Know, then, that I have no need of their cemetery, I spit on it. All my life you've persecuted me, you're all my enemies.

DU CROISY: For the love of God, maître, we...

LA GRANGE: *(To* BOUTON*)* How can he play in such a state, how can he play?

(Whistling and loud noise beyond the curtain)

LA GRANGE: Hear that?

MOLIÈRE: It's carnival-time. They've broken the chandeliers in the Palais-Royal more than once. The parterre is making merry.

BOUTON: *(Sinisterly)* One-eye is in the theater.

(Pause)

MOLIÈRE: *(Growing quiet)* Ah... *(Frightened)* Where's Moirron?

(MOLIÈRE *rushes to* MOIRRON *and hides in his cloak.* MOIRRON, *his teeth bared, says nothing, embraces* MOLIÈRE.)

DU CROISY: *(In a whisper)* We should send for a doctor.

MOLIÈRE: *(Peeking from the cloak, timidly)* He can't touch me onstage, can he?...

(Silence. The door opens and RIVALLE *runs in. She is wearing a peculiar costume, is half naked as usual, on her head a doctor's hat, wheel-like spectacles.)*

RIVALLE: We can't drag out the intermission any more... Either play or...

LA GRANGE: He wants to play, there's nothing we can do.

RIVALLE: *(Looks at* MOLIÈRE *for a long time)* Play.

MOLIÈRE: *(Emerging from the cloak)* Good for you. Come, my brave old girl, I'll kiss you. How can we start the last performance and not finish it? She understands. You've been acting with me for twelve years, and, would you believe it, I've never once seen you dressed. You're always naked.

RIVALLE: *(Kisses him)* Eh, Jean-Baptiste, the king will forgive you.

MOLIÈRE: *(Vaguely)* He...yes...

RIVALLE: Will you listen to me?

ACT FOUR

MOLIÈRE: *(After reflecting)* I will. But not to them. *(Makes an awkward movement with his leg)* They're fools. *(Suddenly gives a start and changes abruptly)* Forgive me, gentlemen, I allowed myself to be rude. I myself don't understand how it escaped me. I'm nervous. Put yourselves in my position. Monsieur du Croisy...

DU CROISY, LA GRANGE, BOUTON: *(In chorus)* We're not angry.

RIVALLE: Right after your last line, we'll lower you through the trap door, hide you in my dressing room till morning, and at dawn you will leave Paris. Agreed? Let's begin, then.

MOLIÈRE: Yes. We'll play the last scene.

(DU CROISY, LA GRANGE, *and* MOIRRON *seize their masks and disappear.* MOLIÈRE *embraces* RIVALLE *and she disappears.* MOLIÈRE *takes off his dressing gown.* BOUTON *opens the curtain that separates us from the stage. On the stage there is an enormous bed, a white statue, a dark portrait on the wall, a bed table with a little bell. The chandeliers are shaded in green, which creates a cozy night light onstage. Candles are lit in a booth, the prompter appears in it. Beyond the main curtain there is the noise of the house. Every now and then a sinister whistle soars up.* MOLIÈRE, *changing abruptly, flits onto the bed with extraordinary lightness, lies down, covers himself with a blanket.)*

MOLIÈRE: *(Whispers to the prompter)* Begin!

(A gong strikes, the house beyond the curtain falls silent. Merry, mysterious music begins to play. MOLIÈRE *snores to it. With a rustle, the enormous curtain opens. It feels as if the theater is overcrowded. In the gilded loge at the edge some vague faces loom up. There is a loud roll of the kettledrum, and from under the floor* LA GRANGE *rises, with an incredible nose, wearing a black cap, and peers into* MOLIÈRE's *face.)*

MOLIÈRE: *(Waking up, terrified)*
By night, and in my bedroom, too?
You devil! Kindly get you gone!

(Music)

LA GRANGE:
Why such an insolent to-do?
It's me, your therapist, Pourgon!

MOLIÈRE: *(Sits up on the bed in fright)*
Sorry. But who's that hiding there?!...

(The portrait on the wall tears open, DU CROISY sticks himself out of it—a drunken mug with a red nose, a doctor's spectacles and cap.)

MOLIÈRE:
Why, here's another, I'm glad to see!

DU CROISY: *(In a drunken bass)*
The ve-ne-ree-o-logical chair
Has sent me here as deputy!

MOLIÈRE:
Am I dreaming? Can it be?!...

(The statue falls to pieces, and RIVALLE flies out of it.)

MOLIÈRE:
What is this wild incident?

RIVALLE:
Of the medical faculty
I am the permanent president.

VOICE: *(In the house)* Ha, ha, ha.

(Out of the floor grows a monster—a doctor of unbelievable height.)

MOLIÈRE:
A doctor who goes up two stories!...
Servants! Help! *(Rings)* I'm seeing things!

ACT FOUR

(The pillows on the bed explode, and at the head MOIRRON *emerges.)*

MOIRRON:
It is I, Doctor Diafoirus,
Thomas, the incomparable. Who rings?

(The third curtain falls, the furthest one, and from behind it emerges a chorus of doctors and apothecaries in ridiculous and strange masks.)

MOLIÈRE:
But to what is this honor due?...
It seems the hour is rather late...

RIVALLE:
We have come to you with news!

CHORUS OF DOCTORS: *(Bursts out)*
To be a doctor is your fate!!

RIVALLE:
Who's the one that cures his stomach?

MOLIÈRE:
He who on heaps of rhubarb feasts!

RIVALLE:
Bene, bene, bene, bene.

Chorus of Doctors
Novus doctor dignus est.

DU CROISY:
And what about, say, syphilis?...

MOLIÈRE:
A good eight years on mercury.

VOICE: *(In the house)* Ha, ha, ha.

LA GRANGE:
Bravo, bravo, bravo, bravo,
A remarkable reply!

RIVALLE:
He is truly full of knowledge…

DU CROISY:
It comes tripping off his tongue!

(ONE-EYE *suddenly appears in the loge, sits on the edge, and freezes in a pose of expectation.*)

MOIRRON:
And there in the celestial college…

CHORUS OF DOCTORS:
The doctors he will sit among!!

MOLIÈRE: *(Suddenly falls down comically)* Bring me Madeleine! To advise me… Help!

VOICE: *(In the house)* Ha, ha, ha.

MOLIÈRE: Parterre, don't laugh…quick…quick… *(He lies still.)*

(Music plays a few moments longer, then collapses. In response to the beating of the kettledrum, a spooky NUN emerges in MOLIÈRE's *dressing room.)*

NUN: *(Nasally)* Where's his costumes? *(Quickly gathers all* MOLIÈRE's *costumes and disappears with them.)*

(Commotion on the stage)

LA GRANGE: *(Taking off his mask, at the footlights)* Ladies and gentlemen, Monsieur de Molière, who played the role of Argan, has collapsed… *(Nervously)* The performance cannot be finished.

(Silence. Then:)

VOICE: *(A cry from the loge:)* Give us our money back!

(Whistling, noise.)

MOIRRON: *(Taking off his mask)* Who shouted about money? *(Draws his sword, tries the point)*

ACT FOUR

BOUTON: *(Onstage, in a stifled voice)* Who could have shouted it?

MOIRRON: *(Pointing to the loge)* You or you? *(Silence. To* ONE-EYE*)* Filthy animal!

*(*ONE-EYE*, drawing his sword, climbs onto the stage.)*

MOIRRON: *(Goes cat-like to meet him)* Come on, come on. Closer. *(As he passes* MOLIÈRE*, he looks at him, then sticks his sword into the floor, turns and leaves the stage.)*

(The PROMPTER *in his booth suddenly bursts into tears.* ONE-EYE *looks at* MOLIÈRE*, sheathes his sword, and leaves the stage.)*

LA GRANGE: *(To* BOUTON*)* Close the curtain, will you!

(The CHORUS *comes out of its stupor, the doctors and apothecaries rush to* MOLIÈRE*, surround him in a frightful crowd, and he disappears.* BOUTON *finally closes the curtain, the audience beyond it roars.* BOUTON *runs after the group carrying* MOLIÈRE *away.)*

LA GRANGE: Ladies and gentlemen, help me!
(Speaks through an opening in the curtain.) Ladies and gentlemen, I beg you...go home...something terrible has happened...

RIVALLE: *(At another opening)* Ladies and gentlemen...I beg you...ladies and gentlemen...

(The curtain billows up, the curious try to get on the stage.)

DU CROISY: *(At a third opening)* Ladies and gentlemen... ladies and gentlemen...

LA GRANGE: Put out the lights!

*(*DU CROISY *puts out the lights, knocking the candles down with his sword. The noise in the house dies down a little.)*

RIVALLE: *(At the opening)* Put yourselves in our place, ladies and gentlemen...go home...the performance is over...

(The last candle is put out, and the stage sinks into darkness. Everything vanishes. Light plays on the crucifix. The stage is open, dark, and empty. Not far from Molière's *mirror, a dark figure sits crouched. A lantern floats onto the stage, the dark* La Grange *enters.)*

La Grange: *(In a solemn and stern voice)* Who's still here? Who is it?

Bouton: It's me, Bouton.

La Grange: Why don't you go to him?

Bouton: I don't want to.

La Grange: *(Goes to his dressing room, sits down, lit by the green light, opens the book, speaks and writes)* "February 17th. There was a fourth performance of the play *The Imaginary Invalid,* written by Monsieur de Molière. At ten o'clock in the evening, Monsieur de Molière, while performing the role of Argan, collapsed onstage, and was taken from us at once, without a confession, by inexorable death." *(Pause)* As a token of it, I draw a very big black cross. *(Thinks)* What was the cause of this? What? What shall I write down? Was the king's disfavor the cause of it, or was it the black Cabal?... *(Thinks)* What was the cause? Fate. That's what I'll write down. *(Writes and fades into the darkness)*

(Curtain)

END OF PLAY

www.ingramcontent.com/pod-product-compliance
Lightning Source LLC
Chambersburg PA
CBHW060216050426
42446CB00013B/3089